Frogs in Trouble

By Roger Cantu

Mystic Buddha Publishing House
Copyright © 2024 by Roger Cantu
ISBN: 978-0-9972431-7-8

Once upon a time, two young sibling frogs and an elder frog lived in a pond on the edge of a Buddhist temple.

The frogs lived happily and frolicked around the pond, having a good time.

The elder frog would sing them a happy song before bed every night.

One day, the younger frog said to their sibling. "Let's have a jumping contest!" The older frog happily agreed and started jumping all around.

"Let's make this more fun," said the younger frog. Let's jump through the temple's window!"

"Be careful!" said the older frog. "You don't want to knock anything down."

Once inside, the sibling frogs were looking around the meditation room. A Buddha statue sat on the table.

"I'm going to jump on his head," said the younger frog.

"No, stop messing around. You are going to get us into trouble," said the older frog.

The younger frog jumped on the Buddha's head and knocked it down. When the Buddha hit the ground, his head came off.

"Oh no!" yelled the younger frog panicking. "What are we going to do?"

"Help me move this thing. Maybe we can hide it, and they will never know."

"Are you kidding me?" asked the older frog. "You think they would come in and not notice the Buddha is missing."

The younger frog tried carrying the Buddha, but it was too heavy.

"Help me... the elder frog is going to kill me if he finds out what I did. This is terrible!"

Meanwhile, the elder frog was peacefully meditating, when he started hearing all the racket coming from the temple.

He stood up, jumped through the window, and caught the sibling frogs red-handed.

"What is going on here?" he asked.

The younger frog looked up, tears started pouring out, and made a loud cry.

"Waaaaah, I'm sorry. Please don't tell the monks. They are going fry me and eat me for lunch."

"The monks are vegetarians. They are not going to eat you," said the elder frog. "Now settle down and tell me what happened."

The young frog explained what happened and hoped the elder frog would not be mad.

"Now listen to me," said the elder frog. "You have two choices here. You can think, 'Oh no, I have a problem. The elder frog is going to kill me, or, oh no, I have a problem. I better talk to the elder frog'."

Which one is better?

The young frog understood, winked, and smiled. "Now, help me move the Buddha," said the elder frog.

All three frogs moved the Buddha back to where it belonged.

They jumped to the edge of the window and hid until one of the monks came in.

When a monk came in, he saw the Buddha, picked it up, and thought the wind knocked it down. He grabbed some glue, put the head back on its body, and cleaned it.

When the people came to meditate that evening, they said that the Buddha looked shiny and new.

The three frogs returned to the pond happily, feeling they solved the situation.

"When you have a problem, finding someone you can talk to is a good idea. It could be a teacher, a parent, or an elder you trust," said the elder frog.

"It is better to talk about your problems and seek help than to hide your problems and keep them inside."

"Thank you for your advice, elder frog," said the younger frog.

The frogs returned home. The elder frog sang a happy song, and they frolicked all night long. "Ribbit, ribbit…"

Note to Teachers and Parents

Frogs in Trouble is a simple story with a powerful message. "It is better to talk about your problems and seek help than to hide your problems and keep them inside."

The message relayed in this story is based on an actual incident and told as an allegory. An allegory is a narrative story that conveys a message about life using pictures, characters, and events.

We hope you enjoyed this story and share it with others in your school, families, and friends.

Printed in the USA
CPSIA information can be obtained
at www.ICGtesting.com
JSHW062353090424
60886JS00006B/40